EARLY LEARNING

For three- to five-year-o

Raggy Blanket Holiday

Story by Pie Corbett
Activities by David Bell, Pie Corbett
Geoff Leyland and Mick Seller

Illustrations by Diann Timms

Mum   Dad

Baby

Jenny

For Marius

This year,
Baby took raggy blanket
on holiday.

Jenny took Little Brown Bear.

Look at Baby's blanket.

What shapes can you see?

Point to the circles, the triangles and the squares.

Take a piece of paper and make your own pattern for a blanket full of shapes and colours.

The beach was hot and sandy.
We played in the rock pools.

Look at the picture and talk about all the different things you could find on the beach.

If you can, make a collection of shells or pebbles.

Sort them according to their size. Which is the biggest and which is the smallest?

Can you sort them by their colour?

We paddled with Dad
and went to the
seaside shop.

FUNNY GLASSE
£2·50

SWEETS
10 P

SUMMER
SPECIAL

COMICS 20P

HATS 50P

SPADES
£1·50

The shop is full of things to buy.

Can you read the prices?

What could you buy if you had 10p?

What could you buy if you had 20p?

What is the most expensive thing
that you could buy?

We built sandcastles
and rode on the donkeys.

Can you see any patterns in the sand where people have walked?

Do you think that the sand is wet or dry?

Draw some circles in some clean, dry sand on an old tray, and then in some clean, wet sand.

What did you notice?

We watched Punch and
Judy and went for a train ride.

Do you know the Punch and Judy story?

When you next visit the library with someone, see if you can find a book with the story in it.

Have you ever been on a train ride?

Draw a train full of all your friends and family.

Can you make a pattern out of bridge shapes? They look like the letter 'n' or 'm'.

At tea-time we went back to
Mrs Jenkins' guest house.

We had fish and chips.

Can you remember everything that has happened so far?

What happened first?
What happened next?

What was the last thing the family did before coming to the guest house?

After tea, Mum said we could play quietly.

Baby wanted a story.

What story would you tell Baby?

Make up a story about Baby doing something naughty. Perhaps it could be a holiday story.

Can you remember any fairy stories? Try drawing your favourite part of it.

But we couldn't find
raggy blanket anywhere!

Perhaps we had left it on
the beach?

Sometimes it's difficult to remember where
or when you last saw something.
Here's a game to test your memory.

Ask a grown-up to help you to make six pairs
of cards to show things you might find on
the beach. You could draw shells, crabs,
seaweed, fish, sand and pebbles, for example.

Place the 12 cards face down.

Take it in turns to turn over two cards.
If you pick up two the same, you keep them.
The winner is the person with most cards at
the end of the game.

We ran back to the beach, but...

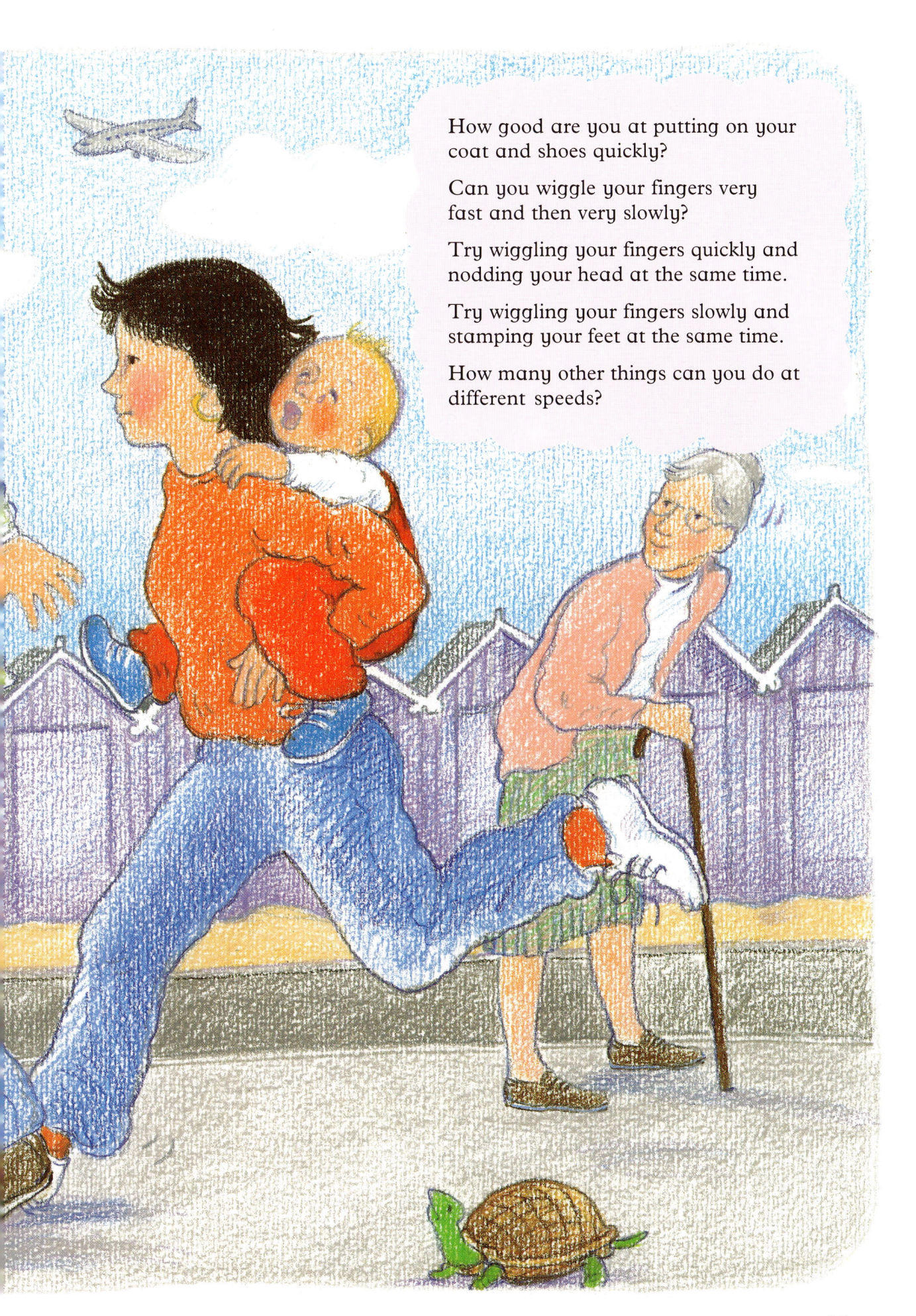

How good are you at putting on your coat and shoes quickly?

Can you wiggle your fingers very fast and then very slowly?

Try wiggling your fingers quickly and nodding your head at the same time.

Try wiggling your fingers slowly and stamping your feet at the same time.

How many other things can you do at different speeds?

What can you see on the sea?

What can you see under the surface of the sea?

Who is coming out of the sea?

Remember to take care whenever you play near the sea.

Baby was very sad.

Dad bought us an ice-cream,
but it was no good.

Talk about some things that make you sad.

Draw or paint a sad face.

Draw some sad and happy mouths.

Try to make patterns using these shapes.
They look like 'n' or 'u'.

Mrs Jenkins gave Baby a hanky
to suck but it was no good.

Find six of your favourite toys.

Can you tell which is which just by touching them?

With someone else, take it in turns to close your eyes and to feel your toy, just using your hands.

Is it rough or smooth, hard or soft? Think up as many words as you can to tell the other person what the toy is like.

Now close your eyes and gently touch different hands in your family. Tell the person what you can feel as you are touching them.

Jenny gave Baby
Little Brown Bear to cuddle
in bed, but it was no good.

26

What would you give Baby to cheer him up?
Perhaps you could sing a nursery rhyme.

Tell him about something funny that has
happened to you to make him feel better.

Then Mum had an idea which sent
her running through the streets...

Poor Mum has had to run all the way back to the sea front.

Take care, Mum, don't fall down the steps!
Point to and count the steps.
How many are there for Mum to go down?

If you have any steps at home, you could count them too.

DECK CHAIRS
£1
PER DAY

...back to the seaside shop where she'd bought a pair of joke glasses, and the shopkeeper gave her a little raggy blanket that someone had left behind.

Can you name the different things for sale?

How much does each one cost?

Try to read the prices on the labels -
you might need some help.

Arrange some of your toys into a shop display.
Make price labels for them.

What do you think Baby and Jenny will say when
they see the raggy blanket again?

Activity Notes

Pages 2-3 Children need to be able to distinguish between different two-dimensional shapes. Allow children to describe for themselves the different characteristics of the shapes and to spot similar shapes around them.

Pages 4-5 If you don't have any shells, you could use pasta shapes, beans, etc. Sorting things using one criteria such as colour is the first step towards an understanding of classification - an important scientific concept. Encourage further close observation by pressing the shells into a sheet of soft modelling clay to make patterns and pictures.
Warn children of the danger of putting small objects into their mouths.

Pages 6-7 Children are soon able to recognise simple prices such as 10p and 20p. Although they won't understand values, they will be able to make a list of things that can be bought for these amounts.

Pages 8-9 Observation is a key scientific skill; develop this skill further by playing 'Guess the Impression'. Make a collection of six familiar toys. Roll out a sheet of modelling clay. Take it in turns to press one of the toys into the modelling clay to leave an impression. Guess which toy has been used.

Pages 10-11 When you visit the library, always let your child choose a book. Learning to make choices is an important part of becoming a reader. Look for old favourites, books by favourite authors or books that are about television characters. Try new books, too.
Early drawings of patterns lead into pencil control and handwriting. Make sure that the bridge shapes are drawn from left to right. If your child is interested in writing letter shapes, ask your playgroup or local infant school for advice.

Pages 12-13 Sequencing events helps children to become aware of the passage of time. Ask them to put in order events which have happened during the day using such words as 'firstly', 'secondly', etc.

Pages 14-15 Making up stories can be great fun with young children. They enjoy stories about themselves and their family and friends. Make sure that whatever happens, everything turns out all right in the end. These sorts of stories help children cope with their feelings.
Reading and telling traditional tales from around the world is an important part of a child's upbringing.

Pages 16-17 Children need to be able to observe similarity and differences in a variety of objects. Extend the game by drawing several different pairs of shells to encourage even closer observation.

Pages 18-19 As children grow, they become increasingly more aware of their own bodies and their capabilities. To develop this awareness still further, try playing a version of 'Simon Says' but use 'Little Brown Bear Says...stand on one leg... do two jumps... wiggle one finger', etc.

Pages 20-21 Positional language such as 'in', 'out', 'under' or 'over' is best used in natural situations. Encourage children to use this language as they follow their daily routine.

Pages 22-23 Encourage your child to invent and use patterns in drawing such as dots, dashes, crosses, circles, U-shapes, N-shapes, slanting lines or half-moon shapes like a C. This early patterning can be fun and develops pencil control which, later on, will make handwriting easier. Keep it fun and don't worry if the patterns look scribbly.

Pages 24-25 Talk about how touch is one of five senses - the others being sight, smell, hearing and taste. Next, close your eyes and try to identify familiar toys by touching them with your feet and then with your hands. Talk about how easy this game is.

Pages 26-27 There are a number of excellent nursery rhyme collections and tapes with traditional rhymes that should be part of all small children's repertoire. Singing together, playing pat-a-cake, knee-bouncing rhymes, This Little Piggy..., tickling rhymes, clapping rhymes and ring games such as 'Ring a Ring a Roses' all help to develop a sense of rhythm, pleasure in language, co-operation and participation.

Pages 28-29 Simple counting activities are all around us and these make much more sense to children than abstract activities on paper. Use practical contexts such as climbing stairs to reinforce simple counting.

Pages 30-31 When you are out shopping, draw your child's attention to the labels and prices. Familiar signs, labels and notices are often the first words a child learns to read. Playing at shops is an early way of appreciating money, weighing and selling. Encourage your child to think about what the characters in the story might feel: this helps to deepen their understanding.